Aunt Lettuce, I Want to Peek Under Your Skirt

Aunt Lettuce, I Want to Peek Under Your Skirt

POEMS BY
Charles Simic

DRAWINGS BY
Howie Michels

A
TIN HOUSE
BLOOMSBURY
BOOK

Published by Bloomsbury Publishing, New York and London
Distributed to the trade by Holtzbrinck Publishers

All papers used by Bloomsbury Publishing are natural, recyclable
products made from wood grown in well-managed forests.
The manufacturing processes conform to the environmental
regulations of the country of origin.

Library of Congress Cataloging-in-Publication Data
has been applied for.

ISBN 1-58234-461-2
ISBN-13 9781582344614

First U.S. Edition 2005

1 3 5 7 9 10 8 6 4 2

Typeset by Palimpsest Book Production Limited,
Polmont, Stirlingshire
Printed in the United States of America
by Quebecor World Fairfield

CONTENTS

AUNT LETTUCE

Aunt Lettuce, I want to peek under your skirt.

LOVE FLEA

He took a flea
From her armpit
To keep

And cherish
In a matchbox,
Even pricking his finger

From time to time
To feed it
Drops of blood.

MARGARET WAS COPYING

Margaret was copying a recipe for "saints roasted with onions" from an old cook book. The ten thousand sounds of the world were hushed so we could hear the scratchings of her pen. The saint was asleep in the bedroom with a wet cloth over his eyes. Outside the window the author of the book sat in a flowering apple tree killing lice between his fingernails.

PRETTY PICTURE

For Kurt Brown

She thought being stark naked
Made her more interesting to cows,
So she strolled over with a glass of red wine
To pay them a visit,
Greeting each one in turn
While they stared at her with bloodshot eyes.

One occasionally saw a fox
Step out of the woods.
Where, where? she cried out,
And set at a trot across the field.
We saw her climb over the wire fence
And start picking daisies.

In the end, we didn't dare call her back,
Worrying it might draw attention
Of the mailman due to drive up any minute.
In the meantime, only the crows
Flying back and forth over our heads
Appeared to be frankly scandalized.

VENUS IN A BATH WITH COCKROACHES

Something spooky about these streets
Where I walked this evening
Past rows and rows of identical buildings,
Their windows either dark or lit
And hung with thick curtains,
Save one where a bald fellow sat eating his dinner
With his nose in his plate,
While his cat watched me go.

Thousands of others hidden from view,
Like the one already undressed
Who waits for a tub to fill with hot water,
Imagination, that devil's helper,
Showed me her heavy breasts
And her narrow hips as I hurried by
With my head tucked into my coat,
Because the wind had chilled me to the bone.

THE SCARECROW

God's refuted but the devil's not.

This year's tomatoes are something to see.
Bite into them, Martha,
As you would into a ripe apple.
After each bite add a little salt.

If the juices run down your chin
Onto your bare breasts,
Bend over the kitchen sink.

From there you can see your husband
Come to a dead stop in the empty field
Before one of his bleakest thoughts
Spreading its arms like a scarecrow.

LOVE WORKER

Diligent solely in what concerns love;
In all else, dilatory, sleep-walking, sullen.
Some days you could not budge me
Even if you were to use a construction crane.
I work only at loving and being loved.
Tell me, people, ain't it right
To lie in bed past noon
Eating fried chicken and guzzling beer?

Consider the many evils thus avoided
While finding new places to kiss
    with greasy lips.
Easier for Schwarzkopf to take Kuwait
Than for us to draw the curtains.
The sky is blue. It must be summer already.
The blind street preacher is shouting down below.
Your breasts and hair are flying—
Like the clouds, the white clouds.

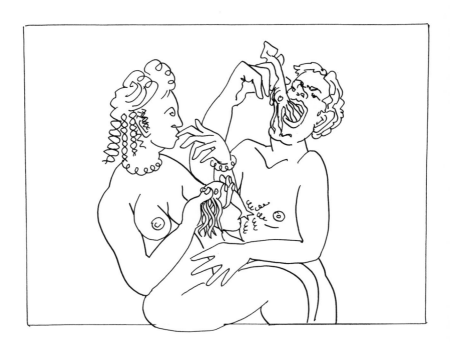

SMALL FEAST

Naked at the table,
Face to face,
Eating grilled squid
With our hands.

She licks olive oil
And garlic
Off her long fingers,
One by one.

Eat some bread, I say.
She just laughs at that,
A hot pepper flake stuck
On the tip of her tongue.

CRAZY ABOUT HER SHRIMP

We don't even take time
To come up for air.
We keep our mouths full and busy
Eating bread and cheese
And smooching in between.

No sooner have we made love
Than we are back in the kitchen.
While I chop the hot peppers,
She wiggles her ass
And stirs the shrimp on the stove.

How good the wine tastes
That has run red
Out of a laughing mouth!
Down her chin
And onto her naked tits.

"I'm getting fat," she says,
Turning this way and that way
Before the mirror.
"I'm crazy about her shrimp!"
I shout to the gods above.

EASTERN EUROPEAN COOKING

While Marquis de Sade had himself buggered—
O just around the time the Turks
Were roasting my ancestors on spits,
Goethe wrote "The Sorrows of Young Werther."

It was chilly, raw, down-in-the-mouth
We were slurping bean soup thick with smoked sausage,
On 2nd Avenue, where years before I saw an old horse
Pull a wagon piled up high with flophouse mattresses.

Anyway, as I was telling my uncle Boris,
With my mouth full of pig's feet and wine:
"While they were holding hands and sighing under
    parasols,
We were being hung by our tongues."

"I make no distinction between scum,"
He said, and he meant everybody,
Us and them: A breed of murderers' helpers,
Evil-smelling torturers' apprentices.

Which called for another bottle of Hungarian wine,
And some dumplings stuffed with prunes,
Which we devoured in silence
While the Turks went on beating their cymbals and drums.

Luckily we had this Transylvanian waiter,
A defrocked priest, ex–dancing school instructor,
Regarding whose excellence we were in complete agreement
Since he didn't forget the toothpicks with our bill

LOVE TALK

The truth is, we are nearer to heaven
Every time we lie down.
If you doubt me, look at the cat
Rolled over with its feet in the air.

A sunny morning after a storm
Is one more invitation to paradise.
So we leapt out of bed together
Having every intention to dress quickly.

Only to dally naked
Giving each other little pecks
As we buzzed with love talk
Edging our way back to bed.

THE INVITATION

We are going to serve a late lunch
For a few friends in the garden.
We'll start with cold squid salad,
A pot of black and green olives
And a loaf of homemade bread to wipe
The garlic and oil off our plates
When we are not sipping the wine.

And if some bird graciously assents
To chirp for us after the grilled lamb,
The cheese and the wild blueberries,
We'll raise our glasses and toast
The golden light between the leaves,
The shadows lengthening,
And keep them raised till the song is over.

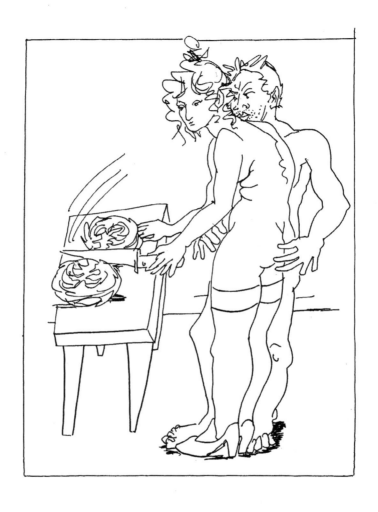

CABBAGE

She was about to chop the head
In half,
But I made her reconsider
By telling her:
"Cabbage symbolizes mysterious love."

Or so said one Charles Fourier,
Who said many other strange and wonderful things,
So that people called him mad behind his back,

Whereupon I kissed the back of her neck
Ever so gently,

Whereupon she cut the cabbage in two
With a single stroke of her knife.

CAFÉ PARADISO

My chicken soup thickened with pounded young almonds
My blend of winter greens.
Dearest tagliatelle with mushrooms, fennel, anchovies,
Tomatoes and vermouth sauce.
Beloved monkfish braised with onions, capers,
And green olives.
Give me your tongue tasting of white beans and garlic,
Sexy little assortment of formaggi and frutta!
I want to drown with you in red wine like a pear,
Then sleep in a macédoine of wild berries and cream.

BEAUTY

I'm telling you, this was the real thing, the same
one they kicked out of Aesthetics, told her she didn't
exist!

O you simple, indefinable, ineffable, and so forth.
I like your black apron, and your new Chinese girl's
hairdo. I also like naps in the afternoon, well-chilled
white wine, and the squabbling of philosophers.

What joy and happiness you give us each time you
reach over the counter to take our money, so we catch
a whiff of your breath. You've been chewing on
sesame crackers and garlic salami, divine creature!

When I heard the old man, Plotinus, say something
about "every soul wanting to possess you," I gave him
a dirty look, and rushed home to unwrap and kiss the
pink ham you sliced for me with your own hand.

TOUCHED BY SOMETHING HIGHER

A hateful little creep,
Disreputable, mean and perverse,
I'm looking for someone like you,
Touched by something higher
And still crazy enough to hope
That even greater bliss
Awaits her in sexual wilderness
With a hairy-backed beast
Reduced nowadays to sipping muscatel
On a park bench
And leering with nervous twitch
At every woman who happens by.

THE SEERESS

You'll lead a saint into wickedness,
Her cards say.
The breasts about to slip out of her dress
Worthy of a séance all their own.

Oh my storefront seeress,
With your moist, roving tongue
That warns of unhappiness
Which is a secret happiness.

AT THE COOKOUT

The wives of my friends
Have the air
Of having shared a secret.
Their eyes are lowered
But when we ask them
What for
They only glance at each other
And smile,
Which only increases our desire
To know . . .

Something they did
Long ago,
Heedless of the consequences,
That left
Such a lingering sweetness?

Is that the explanation
For the way
They rest their chins

In the palms of their hands,

Their eyes closed

In the summer heat?

Come tell us,

Or give us a hint.

Trace a word or just a single letter

In the wine

Spilled on the table.

MY BELOVED

after D. Khrams

In the fine print of her face
Her eyes are two loopholes.
No, let me start again.
Her eyes are flies in milk,
Her eyes are baby Draculas.

To hell with her eyes.
Let me tell you about her mouth.
Her mouth's the red cottage
Where the wolf ate grandma.

Ah, forget about her mouth,
Let me talk about her breasts.
I get a peek at them now and then
And even that's more than enough
To make me lose my head,
So I better tell you about her legs.

When she crosses them on the sofa
It's like the jailer unwrapping a parcel
And in that parcel is a Christmas cake
And in that cake a sweet little file
That gasps her name as it files my chains.

STRAY DOGS

The way we stripped and embraced in that field,
Three stray dogs came by
To see what our moaning was all about.
I saw their worried eyes
As I parted your legs with kisses.

And then your tongue went around mine,
And you pulled my hair till it hurt,
And there were broken blue flowers
Under your white ass and the mutts
Sniffing all around us in wonder

PRETTY WATCHBAND

Feeding ladybugs
To a rattlesnake
Out of your own hand,
Miss Muffet.

Your watchband made me think of that,
And your naked breast and nipple
Made me think of milk
For the darting tongue to lick,
And the hidden equally busy
Tiny red teeth of your watch to nibble.

SUFFERING FOR A CAUSE

Since our life's nothing but a long probation,
We won't heed the one getting ready
To sunbathe topless in the neighbor's yard.
We'll stay in the corner all day.
Break silence only to speak to a cat.

We'll follow the example of holy martyrs,
Who elevate their horniness
So they only see angels
As they make do on a diet of bread and water
On the bare floor of their cells.

May prayer lift us above the dark treetops
In this cloudless summer afternoon.
We won't stir, we won't go and peek
If she's still there on the same red blanket,
Oiling her sunburned breasts.

The curtains lift teasingly at the window,
The brandy—not to be touched—
Glares, red-eyed
From a snifter on the dining room table
As dust motes frolic in the golden sunlight

ST. GEORGE AND THE DRAGON

When Queen Money
Sits naked in my lap,
And her fat bulldog
Comes to growl

While she rides me
Like a horsey
Using her long red hair
As a whip,

And the ceiling at midday
Is a lush maze
Of tree shadows
Tangling and untangling themselves,

And all that comes to mind
Is St. George rearing up
With a lance to slay
The fire-spitting dragon.

TRANSPORT

In the frying pan
On the stove
I found my love
And me naked.

Chopped onions
Fell on our heads
And made us cry.
It's like a parade,
I told her, confetti
When some guy
Reaches the moon.

"Means of transport,"
She replied obscurely
While we fried.
"Means of transport!"

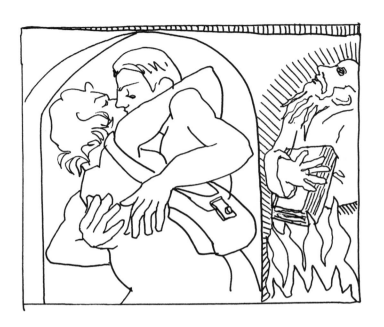

MARTHA'S PURSE

No sooner had I thought of her
And closed my eyes to recall a kiss,
And some other shenanigans
That left us rumpled and breathless,
When the memory of her purse,
The one she used to dangle over her arm
And carry everywhere she went,
Came to intrude between us again.

What's in it? I must've asked
And got no sensible reply.
It had a silver clasp like a strongbox
That hurt when I pressed her close,
That one time against a church wall,
A breath away, surely, from some holy martyr
Tactfully staring at the ceiling
While being licked over by flames.

NUDES IN A MUSEUM
For Howie

They like being stared at
By lone men
And large groups of visitors
Wearing headphones.

They part their lips a bit,
Stick their boobs out further,
Let their fingers wander
Down to their crotches.

Only the young girls
And the guards on duty
Keep their eyes lowered
As they walk past

Like shamefaced fathers
Shielding their daughters
Whose older sisters
Hold court in a brothel.

A NOTE ON THE AUTHOR

Charles Simic published his first book in 1967 and since has written more than sixty books of poetry and prose. Born in Belgrade, he is considered one of the greatest American poets of our time. He received the Pulitzer Prize for *The World Doesn't End* in 1990, and his 1996 collection, *Walking the Black Cat*, was a finalist for the National Book Award for Poetry.

A NOTE ON THE ILLUSTRATOR

Howie Michels is a painter and illustrator whose work has been exhibited widely. He most recently illustrated *The Porcupine's Kisses*, by poet Stephen Dobyns.

A NOTE ON THE TYPE

This old-style face is named after the Frenchman Robert Granjon, a sixteenth-century letter cutter whose italic types have often been used with the romans of Claude Garamond. The origins of this face, like those of Garamond, lie in the late-fifteenth-century types used by Aldus Manutius in Italy.